I remember my name

Poetry by
Samah Sabawi, Ramzy Baroud, Jehan Bseiso

Artwork by David Borrington
Editor – Vacy Vlazna

www.novum-publishing.co.uk

	© 2016 novum publishing
All rights of distribution, including film, radio, television, photomechanical reproduction, sound carrier, electronic media and reprint in extracts, are reserved. Printed in the European Union, using environmentally-friendly, chlorine-free and acid-free paper.	ISBN 978-3-99048-390-9 Editor: Nicola Ratcliff Cover photo: David Borrington Cover design, layout & typesetting: novum publishing Illustrations: David Borrington (9) Author's photo: David Borrington **www.novum-publishing.co.uk**

CONTENTS

Foreword 9

SAMAH SABAWI.. 13
Statuses and Headlines 15
A Confession 17
Imra'a 20
Liberation Anthem 23
Defying the Universe 26
Verses and Spices 28
Words 30
Against the tide 33
God Forsaken 35
Invisible 37
Tales of a city by the sea 39

DR RAMZY BAROUD 43
To Afzal Guru 45
Sand and Tears 49
Illusions 50
Nakba 51
La Cafet 52
Where are the noble poets of Santiago? 53
Lullaby 56
Breathing 58
Open your eyes 60
My name is Herman Wallace 62
Your Body is a Map of the World's Collective Shame 63

JEHAN BSEISO 65
Gaza, from the Diaspora 67
Gaza, from the Diaspora 69

Re: Cemeteries in Palestinian camps
short on space/Daily Star/16.05.12* 73
Brainstorming Nakba 74
VI 75
Postcards 76
Tata's lovesong 77
Gaza, 2009 79
Birth at the Checkpoint 81
Writing Syria 83
Letter to Ghassan Kanafani on the
66th Anniversary of the Nakba 85
Sartor Resartus or The Tailor Re-Tailored 87
Ceasefire 88
Hashtag Gaza 89

Dr VACY VLAZNA 91
DAVID BORRINGTON 93
Glossary 95

DEDICATION

For the besieged who taught the world the meaning of freedom We dedicate this to those who resisted, the ones who treated the injured and the ones who buried their dead under the shelling. This is for the children who lost their parents, and the parents who will not see their children again. We dedicate this book to the city that has become a legend. To Gaza, Palestine.

FOREWORD

I remember my name, is a compelling contribution to Arabic literature and shares with you the deeply personal and deeply political expressions of three gifted Palestinian poets in exile from Gaza: Samah Sabawi, Ramzy Baroud and Jehan Bseiso.

Although Samah, Ramzy and Jehan have distinctive styles, they possess in common incisive intellects, finely tuned by a sense of justice inherent in the Palestinian experience and in their love for Palestine particularly besieged and suffering Gaza.

Samah's poetic style is passionate, lyrical and luminous. She intuitively weaves the most intimate and the political in a magnanimity for reconciliation:

What passed through my womb though precious…
Is not distinct
A beautiful human baby of flesh and blood
No different to that born by the 'other'
There is no 'us' and 'them'

Ramzy's art is grounded in justice for Palestine, yet the fierce intellectual refinement and range of his poetry knows no borders in its fusion of the personal within the global and universal:

And just when you think I am defeated,
My fist will rise from the charred earth,
In a painting by Naji Ali,
Through the thick walls of Louisiana State Penitentiary
In the streets of Hanoi,
Amid the rubble of a Gaza mosque.
Even on my dying bed.

Seemingly freestyle, Jehan's innovative panache is precise and vivid, with a dramatic immediacy cut on an edge of defiance, irony and acuity:

Israeli soldier puts his weapon down to help Um Ali spread her legs, her face is red with shame, her husband is waiting at home in Abu Dis, he doesn't have the right papers with the blue and white stamps, he can't cross to Jerusalem.

The international community is having 9 course dinners in the Alps.

(In the room the women come and go, talking about the status quo).

While their roots are in Gaza, their life journeys, typical of Palestinian refugees, are painfully scattered across the world.

The refugee journey of Samah Sabawi, daughter of the prestigious Gazan poet and author, *Abdul Karim Sabawi,* has spanned Jordan, Canada and her present home in Melbourne, Australia. Her every footstep is an eloquent act of resistance.

Born in Gaza to Nakba refugees from Beit Daras, Ramzy Baroud, like his father, is a freedom fighter now living in Seattle, USA. Ramzy's art of resistance is indefatigable and prodigious.

The Bseiso family ancestry is traced back to 17th century Gaza. Jehan Bseiso, a popular and spirited voice of resistance among the younger generation, was born in Los Angeles, her childhood was in Jordan. She was a university student in Beirut and is now a humanitarian aid worker living in Cairo.

All three poets enjoy high literary profiles in the West and the Middle East: Samah, is an author, playwright, poet and political commentator, Ramzy is an author, poet, editor and political commentator and Jehan is a poet and political commentator. All three are highly respected and renowned Palestinian activists.

I remember my name, welcomes accomplished London artist David Borrington as Artistic Editor. His heightened sensitivity to the poets' vision delivers a powerful visual accompaniment to nine of the poems.

David's aesthetic cover depicts the courageous Red Crescent volunteers carrying the wounded during the 2014 Israel's Operation Protective Edge war on Gaza and the abandoned doll is a touching testimonial to the innocence of Palestine's martyrs.

Enjoy!

Vacy Vlazna
Editor

# SAMAH SABAWI

I am a Palestinian-Canadian-Australian writer, commentator and playwright. More significantly, I am a proud mother of three and the daughter of proud Palestinian parents. I have shared more than half of my life with my husband of 26 years, whose love has helped me heal my wounds and spread my wings. I travelled the world and lived in its far corners, yet always felt haunted by the violence and injustice perpetrated against the poor, the marginalized, the colonized and stateless. No matter where I was, or how vast the world appeared around me, I always felt as though I remained trapped in my place of birth Gaza. The war torn besieged and isolated strip shaped my understanding of my identity and my humanity. So what else could I do but to indulge in Palestine's overwhelming presence and to succumb to telling its stories of humanity's triumphs and tribulations through my art and my poetry?

I have written and produced the plays *Cries from the Land* and *Three Wishes*; both successfully staged in Canada in 2003 and 2008, and my third play, *TALES OF A CITY BY THE SEA* enjoyed a sold-out world premiere run at Melbourne's La Mama Theatre in Australia, an Arabic premiere at Alrowwad's Cultural Theater Society in Palestine and was selected for the Victorian Certificate of Education Drama & Theatre studies' 2016 playlist in Australia. My essays, opeds and poems have been published in various media outlets and my poetry featured in several magazines and books including *With Our Eyes Wide Open: Poems of the New American Century* (West End Press) and *Gaza Unsilenced* (Just World Books). My play *Tales of a City by the Sea* will be published in a stand-alone copy by Currency Press, and as part of an anthology I have co-edited for the Playwrights Canada Press, Canada's major publisher for drama works, *Double Exposure: Plays of the Jewish and Palestinian Diasporas.*

I have received an Australian Postgraduate Award to undertake a PhD by creative project at Victoria University commencing 2016.

STATUSES AND HEADLINES

Words scatter…
Attention span expands between statuses and headlines
I frame my perils of wisdom on cyber walls
I denounce…I declare…I divulge my soul
I offer solidarity
And pass verdicts like delusional royalty
My virtual life … a parody
My profile page, my imaginary throne.

Newsfeed filled with corpses
Attention span expands between statuses and headlines
I protest discrimination famines and wars
140* characters to tear down the walls
140 characters to stop genocide
140 characters to expose a politician who lied
140 characters to give voice to the voiceless
To affirm a life branded worthless…
Nameless children die everyday
Nameless mothers grieve everyday
Nameless fathers bury their sons everyday
Nameless mass graves are dug everyday
Nameless insignificant refugees threaten our peace of mind
Nameless faceless detainees out of sight out of mind
Nameless women sell their bodies
Sell their organs
Sell their babies to survive
No dignity in poverty
Populations stripped of humanity
Only atrocities have names

'Protective Edge'
'Enduring Freedom'
'Cast Lead'
'Desert Shield'
'Pillar of Clouds'
Military operations idealized
Minds stalled paralyzed
War on terror
War of terror
War for terror…
Terror…terror…terror…TERROR…
We grow numb…desensitized
Newsfeed jammed with hasbaranites**
Government agents paid for lies
They 'like' and 'share' what we despise

Morals in peril
Attention span expands between statuses and headlines
140 characters to liberate Palestine
140 characters for gender equality
140 characters to raise money for charity
140 characters…I am wearing thin
140 characters…where do I begin?

Thoughts scatter
Attention span expands
BEYOND statuses and headlines

* Twitter limits tweet length to 140 characters.
** Hasbaranites is a made up word derived from the Israeli word hasbara – propaganda

A CONFESSION

I stand between shame and relief
I breathe
The missiles missed this time
Truth is they didn't really miss
Someone's house is destroyed
But not the house I know so well
Someone's family is grieving
But not the one whose name I carry
I linger…between shame and relief
I breathe…I… breathe…
I tell myself
'This flesh torn and scattered is not flesh I have ever embraced'
I soothe myself
'Nor are these small lifeless hands the ones with a crayon I've traced'
I breathe…
This time the missiles missed
Those whose names are engraved on my lips
This time they didn't stop
Those hearts beating in my chest
They live…and I breathe
But I must confess
Every time the bombs fall I want answers
Where did they strike?
Which street did they blow up?
What neighbourhood did they destroy?
Which lives did they steal?

Aware of my guilt I whisper a prayer:
Dear God, please don't let it be the ones I know
Dear God, please don't let it be the ones I love
Dear God...
Ya allah...ya allah...ya allah...
And when it's over
And while a less fortunate family weeps
I stand between shame and relief
I breathe...
I... breathe...
Thank God my loved ones were spared
This time

January 3, 2009

IMRA'A

For my sisters in the Arab World and beyond
Feb 17, 2013

I
am
woman
Imra'a
Whole
Not a fragment of your shadow
Not a rib torn out of your torso
Not a mail order
Not a house slave
Not a fairy-tale princess
Not a damsel in distress
Not a genie in a bottle
Not a devil
Nor a saint
Not scattered
Not arranged
Not lacking in brain or piety
Not a fountain of propriety
I am eternity
Lived in an instant
I am constant randomness
I am chaos in stability
In songs you ache for me
I am your refuge and your refugee
Your barren desert and your fertile field
Your homeland…your 'watan'
My womb yields the fruit of life
I am your Mother

Daughter
Sister
Wife
A prince of poetry wrote of me
"Alommo madrasaton…"
A mother is a school if well prepared
You prepare a well-mannered nation
For a thousand and one Arabian nights
I am inspiration
In the Holy Scriptures
I am temptation
I am your Eve in the Garden of Eden
My qualities revealed in the holy Quran
'inna kaydahonna azeem'
I am your dream
Your 'hoor alayn'
Your seduction
Your redemption
Your struggle
Your salvation
I am strength and weakness
Rolled into one
I am your lived reality
And all that you refuse to see
I am what you cannot define
Cannot confine
To a fantasy

I am human
Of flesh and blood
My faults monumental
My virtues unquantifiable
I am neither a reflection of you nor on you
Your ticket to paradise does not begin with my virtue
Your peace of mind does not begin with my conformity
Your redemption does not begin with my submission
Your honor is not defined by my chastity
Your fantasies are your own
Your vice is yours alone
For I carry my own
Burden alone
I am woman
Imra'a
Whole

LIBERATION ANTHEM

To the people of Israel who fear our freedom: Don't be afraid, we will liberate you too.

This is my rendition of an anthem to be sung
That day you and I will stand side by side
Shoulder to shoulder
Watching a new dawn wipe away decades of hate and savagery
The day I rise from the ruins of your oppression
I promise you I will not rise alone
You too will rise with me
You will be liberated from your tyranny
And my freedom will bring your salvation

This is my rendition of an anthem to be sung
I'll craft new words of expressions
Outside of this suffocating language that has occupied me
Your words are like your walls
They encroach on my humanity
I am more than demography
I am not your moderate
Not your terrorist
Not your Islamist
Fundamentalist
Extremist
Militant
Radical
I am more than adjectives letters and syllables
I will construct my own language
And defeat your words of power
With the power of my words

This is my rendition of an anthem to be sung
I don't want to obliterate nor humiliate you
I refuse to hate you
Don't care to demonize or proselytize or theorize your intention
Every breath you draw reminds me you are human
The sound of your beating heart is rhythm familiar to my ears
You and I are no different
We are made of blood and tears

This is my rendition of an anthem to be sung
I will rise and soar above your matrix of control
With the strength of my will your walls will fall
And this concrete that segregates us will be used to rebuild homes
Your bulldozers and tanks will dissolve into the earth
The sap will run in the olive trees
The gates will open wide for the refugees
We will be free
I will be your equal
And only then you will be mine
My other self
My fellow human being

June 27, 2011

DEFYING THE UNIVERSE

To my beloved husband Monir

Are your loved ones trapped behind the wall
Do they need the army's permission
For their prayers to reach the sky
For their love to cross the ocean
And touch your thirsty heart
Are your loved ones trapped

Do you yearn to be in your family home
And when you call do they always say:
"we are fine, alhamdollelah"
Does it surprise you that they are whole
While you… are broken
Must they always worry about you
Urge you to have faith in your exile
Must they always pity you
For not breathing the air of your ancestors' land
Must they always comfort you
Even when the bombs are falling
Do you ever wonder who is walled in
Is it you…or is it them
And when it finally dawns upon you their
dignity sets them free
Do you feel ashamed of your liberty

Are your loved ones trapped behind the wall
Do they tell you stories of how they survive
The trees they've replanted…the homes
they've rebuilt
Do they assure you life goes on
Old men still fiddle with their prayer beads
Mothers still bake mamoul on eid
Families still gather under the canopies
With loaded bunches of grapes dangling
above their heads
They nibble on watermelon seeds
They drink meramiah tea
Women still perfect the art of match-making
Men still dream of freedom and democracy
Children still climb on a sycamore tree
Lovers still woo in secrecy
And no matter how the conditions are adverse
Do your loved ones defy the universe
Your loved ones defy the universe

VERSES AND SPICES

Growing up
My father's poems ran through my veins like blood
A necessary life ingredient
A rhythm that kept my heart pumping
Growing up
My mother's cooking nourished my soul
It penetrated every fibre of my being
My Palestinian identity was shaped by food and poetry
By succulent words carefully arranged on the kitchen table
And a feast of verses and spices that lingered in the heart

But of late
My father's poems seem to come out broken
Fatigue has crept into the mind of a man
Who has waited for too long
Of late…
The aroma of my mother's cooking no longer lingers in the air
A sense of ageing…a touch of despair
Time is running out
And still they're trapped so far away from home
Strangers to the ground on which they tread

I look beneath my feet
I too stand in a vast land
Of aspirations not fulfilled
Dreams not accomplished
Desires relentless…unforgotten
Sometimes I am confronted
By the deplorable display of inhumanity
That forced millions away from home
And denied their right to return

I hold on to my identity
I write poetry
And pray its rhythm will keep my children's hearts pumping
I bring out the spices
I carefully measure my cumin, my cardamom
My sumac and cinnamon
I want to fill the air with a defiant aroma
That will nourish my children's souls
And remind them where we come from

I write and I cook
I create a Palestinian feast of delicious verses
For all the parents who have waited for so long

I write and I cook
And hope my pen doesn't dry out
And my spices linger for a while longer
Until I satisfy this hunger
For justice

I tell my children we must be patient
My generation yielded revolutions
But revolutions take generations to yield
So let me teach you how to write and cook
How to live and hope
For a future
Where Palestinians will no longer wait
For freedom, justice
And the simple right to go home!

May 22, 2012

WORDS

Words...
I stand dispossessed
No congress behind me
No statesmen surround me
No lobby to breathe hellfire
No media eager to appease
No three-ring circus
Of intellectual jesters
Academic clowns
And policy experts
Who truly do not see the big elephant in the tent
No legal acrobats dance for me
On a thin rope of decency
No politicians juggle oppression and human rights
On my behalf
No trips to boost careers for MPs and their wives
No propaganda movies
No radio broadcasts
No myths
No lies
No hasbaranites
No army,
No country
Not even one leader to believe in
All I have are my words
To tell my story
My voice to demand justice
And you're telling me
My language is too strong

You may perfect the skill of delusion
The talent of denial
You may express regret and lament
And cry tears of indignation
You may insist you're on my side
But without naming the crimes they commit
Without saying 'Ethnic Cleansing' and 'Apartheid'
Your words ring hollow

So let me hold on to my words
I use them sparingly
I utter one word and a house is resurrected from memory
On a hill in Palestine
I utter another … and I am in a courtyard
Under a sycamore tree
And another
And the scent of Jasmine fills the air
Words
Lift me up from despair
And take me home
Words
Disarm tyrants
Bring down empires
And reveal all the oppressors wish to conceal
Humanity!

I stand dispossessed of everything but my words
They are words of truth
Of fire and steel
I use them deliberately
Not to incite hatred
Not to frighten
But to lighten up this darkness
That tore me into 11 million pieces
And scattered me across the earth
Words tell my story
Nakba
Naksa
Forced exile
Ethnic cleansing
Apartheid
Words
Carefully chosen
Purposely uttered
These are the words that lay the foundation
Of the language of my liberation

AGAINST THE TIDE

I will not be polarized
I will not be polarized
I will not be polarized
I will not be fractionized
Tribalized
Sectarianized
Colonized and fragmented
Like a heartbroken nation
I will not be moved by hatred
Or blindly pick a side
And hide behind a well crafted slogan
I will not place my trust in demagogy
I will embrace ideas not ideology
An enemy of my enemy when a tyrant
Is my enemy
Choosing the best of two evils
Is choosing evil
I will not fall for this game
Of demonizing an entire people
I will not delight when pain is inflicted
on another
I will not close my eyes to inhumanity
I will defend my enemy's rights
Because freedom is not a commodity
To be had by some and denied to others

I will not delight in the suffering
Even of those who oppress me
More importantly
I will trust my maternal instinct
What passed through my womb though precious...
Is not distinct
A beautiful human baby of flesh and blood
No different to that born by the 'other'
There is no 'us' and 'them'
Every death will be mourned by a grieving mother
Her tears... more precious than any flag
I will not be polarized

GOD FORSAKEN

In the aftermath of Israel's bombardment of Gaza, codenamed Cast Lead in 2008–2009, in which more than 1400 Palestinians were killed , most of them women and children. Some IDF soldiers wore t-shirts depicting a pregnant Palestinian woman with her belly in the crosshairs of a rifle with the caption '1shot two kills'

What is a life worth
A grain of earth
A drop of oil
A flag on a hill of holy soil
A cross…a star…a crescent moon…
Is it worth ending a life too soon
What sacred verses can explain
Sniper fire and white phosphorus rain
What Holy Scriptures gave the command
"Thou shall wipe out their villages
And scorch their land"

And after the massacre
Did they lament
Did they seek forgiveness
Did they repent
Did they sanctify their burdened souls
For besieging a people behind their walls
Or did they wear with pride their murderous skills:
A pregnant woman with the caption
"1 SHOT 2 KILLS"

No rest for the less sacred
No safety... no light
No benediction... no prayer...no end in sight
No bread...no medicine...no shelter...no salvation
No angels can survive
This holy Occupation
TELL ME THIS:
What is the life of a Palestinian worth
On this God forsaken earth?

April, 2009

INVISIBLE

This one is for all the little girls who feared walking in the street, even when their mothers held their hand. This one is for all the little girls who begged to hide behind the veil but were told they were too young. This one is for all the little girls who had to grow up fast. This one is for all the little girls who carried their scars for life.

When I was a little girl
I wished to be invisible
I wanted to simply dissolve into thin air
Transcend this world to a new dimension
Where no hand can touch me
No eyes can violate me
Or dig deep into my flesh
No unwelcomed gaze
Can reduce my body to a heap of sexual fantasy
In my world of invisibility
No one can impose their lust on my humanity

Decades passed
And still I hold on to this secret fantasy
I lay down at night wondering what bliss it must be
To be unseen…Unheard…Untouched
To be left alone
No longer needing to perfect facial expression
Or give birth to conversation
Or agonize over conducting a symphony
of tired rhythm
Careless sighs…Feminine laughter
Not too vulgar…Not too timid
Everything is laborious

For a woman
Even the sound of breathing…
Sensualized
But invisible
I would have no need to hide my eyes
Or dig my face into the pillow
And scream empty hollow sounds
I keep my words inside of me
Fearing if uttered
Their sharpness would slice my tongue in halves

I escape into the arms of a childhood fantasy
I convince myself I have the power of invisibility
I transcend into a new dimension
Lighter
I shed my skin
Brighter
I shed my flesh
No weight pushing down on me
No external needs overpower my dignity
I am alive
In my invisibility
I embrace my soul
Here I hide for eternity
Inside myself
Here
Now
I own myself
All of me

TALES OF A CITY BY THE SEA

The landscape constantly changes
Only the sea remains the same
Salty…fluid…mysterious…moody
A consistent presence amid the chaos
Its whooshing waves whisper tales
Of occupiers that have come and gone
Crusaders, tyrants and warlords
Riding on their horses
Riding on their Tanks
Riding on their F16 fighter jets
Always riding through
Leaving their footprints and part of their history
Leaving their artefacts and ruins
Leaving fire and debris
Always leaving…
Only the sea remains
A cure for the trail of broken lives left behind
A landmark untouched by human greed and destruction
Oblivious to war occupation and aggression
Defiant to the rules of man
It embraces the shores of a battered city
It makes a mockery
Of those who try to break its spirit
Those who think they can contain
Its one and a half million beating hearts
It laughs in the face of that big iron wall
There is no limit to the sea's audacity

It breaks the siege every day,
One defiant wave at a time
Connecting Gaza to the rest of the world
And connecting the world with the Shati refugee camp

If you stood with your back to Gaza facing the sea
You can imagine you are some place else
Beirut, Barcelona, Alexandria or Santorini
You can dream of the promise of what lays beyond the horizon
Countries, continents the whole world is out there
If only you could ride the sea
If only your body was bullet proof
If only your boat was made of steel
If only your dream was real

The landscape will change once more
Only the sea will remain the same
Its whooshing waves will whisper new tales
Of occupiers that have come and gone

June 2010

DR RAMZY BAROUD

I was born in a refugee camp in Gaza. My first line of creative writing was the opening of a poem in Arabic, written late at night, with no electricity, during an Israeli military curfew. At 19, my first collection of Arabic poems was published in secret at a Gaza printing house in 1991. If I had been caught, I would have spent at least six months in an Israeli prison for writing material hostile to the state of Israel.

I never ceased writing poetry, although my academic and professional life took me in other directions. I am an internationally-syndicated columnist, a media consultant, an author, the founder/editor of the Palestine Chronicle and other media projects around the world. I have contributed to many books and academic journals. My books include *Searching Jenin, The Second Palestinian Intifada* and, my latest volume is *My Father Was a Freedom Fighter: Gaza's Untold Story* (Pluto Press, London). I hold a Ph.D. from the University of Exeter's European Centre for Palestine Studies.

My early identity as a poet stands above all. It accompanied my childhood formation. Now, when words fail me, I resort to poetry. Poetry breaks away from the confines of geography, into a humanist realm, in which Palestine is central, but also a representation of something much bigger and greater than 'conflict' and 'siege' and other reductionist terminology that reduce the face of Palestine into a specific, ever redundant political discourse. To communicate Palestine, but specially Gaza, considering the hurt it is undergoing, to a message so universal in its magnitude, I think, is beautiful, and important. Wherever I am in the world, from Seattle to Chile to South Africa and regardless of which struggle I am involved in, from Mali to the Rohingya, I am always thinking Palestine, even when I am not conscious of it.

TO AFZAL GURU

He climbed the steps briskly,
head held high,
greeted the hangman
with a gentle nod.
His beard grew defiant
as the hood plunged his face
in visible darkness,
he remembered the judge
asking to repeat
alphabets of servitude.
Ignoring the judge,
he roared names
of forefathers who too had died
standing tall like the Himalayas.
He remembered his
mother's tender touch,
his playful son named
after the poet, Ghalib;
his young, exuberant wife
whose mercy pleas went unheeded
in an unforgiving democracy;
faces of friends flashed by
as did houseboats on Dal Lake
the Shalimar
apple orchards in his hometown
his silly dreams
of heaven above
this playground below
where unruly children
refuse to learn

the etiquette of captivity
in rooms with no windows
only high grey walls
where they pumped petrol
into his anus to break him
as they had countless others
of same skin and soul.
His face was the color
of parched earth,
lips never ceased
reciting one last poem,
the hangman swore,
for God's unruly children
to live forever Free.

Note: Many Kashmiris feel that Afzal Guru, convicted of aiding those who attacked India's Parliament, did not receive a fair trail, that his testimony was coerced, he himself did not kill anyone and, hence, many feel the death penalty was a cruel and unusual punishment, to satisfy the "collective conscience" of the World's largest democracy as the Supreme Court of India noted

SAND AND TEARS

No water here, no humanity either;
only footprints our mothers made
crossing the Sahel into Gaza where
men are pained by long memories,
and women plot their return to die.

Wind, weeping all night, made my
eyes dry, yet when I saw yours
I remembered my name, and I was
determined to reach out for
the moon and ride her back to the

beginning of our dreams, my hand
trembling in your firm grasp,
above the last dune where my
desert abruptly ends
and yours maps out a continent.

For a refugee from Mali

ILLUSIONS

I hear you
In an unspoken echo
In a rhythmic silence
In a heart's broken beat

I read you
In cynical poems
In letters that should never have been written
In words not to be read ever

I see you
In my failing memory
In my withering faith
In a surreal place we once hoped to meet

I feel you
On my barren arms
On this cold journey
On a vast shrinking universe

I need you
Because this dream is only a dream
And I worry
I may never wake up

NAKBA

The bones of my ancestors are the foundation
On which the mountains of Galilee stand.

Our ruggedness might not suit your taste
But we inherited the language of trees.

I am the root of a thousand olive trees
A legacy that will grow through my children

I will fight to preserve my essence until my son
Is old enough to inherit his grandmother's *Thoub*

She lost her childhood amidst dying peasants
Before walking the beaten road of exile and hope

Pleading at every checkpoint, she was the face
in her photo
Searching for a home between Haifa and Eternity.

So, don't talk to me about the Pharaoh: My
Father's blood drenched the skin of Jesus

After the Romans caught him at a checkpoint
Hiding a recipe for revolution, and a love poem

And all the love letters of refugee women
Sent to men suspended on crosses

Overlooking the Martyrs Graveyard
Echoing the battle cries of Jaffa.

LA CAFET

On the other side of nowhere
the surreal road curves into oblivion.
I seek solace in Forgetfulness,
bleeding heart faking a smile.

This is not my home,
nor do these words contain clues
on how it can be found
and, then, lost again.

I sit alone staring into a gap
grown wider between anxiety
and despair. Confusion reigns,
or is it clarity, after all?

Your name is not on the list
Time to return to your desolate moon
Where you draw faces of happy kids,
Of women with faces but no names
And erase them to blur reality with hope

Yet, you told me I found my first earth
and my last sky, the lost poetry in between,
and you promised me whispers of pain
a dying mother has for her newborn.

So, I wait at *La Cafet*
trying to unravel my last clue,
to heal all wounds all around
before God returns from war.

WHERE ARE THE NOBLE POETS OF SANTIAGO?

Neruda wrote his Song of Despair, here
his name was not his own. You, too,
changed names as the junta staged a coup,
hid your face behind masks of tears,
denounced your music as Communistic.

Allende, refugee from Gaza,
was killed here for our sins, some say
his own. Mothers searched for their sons
who fled to Antarctica to write poems
encrypting their timeworn words no tricky

dicks cut from Republican cloth
can decrypt, even though, to be fair to
Yankee ingenuity, your father said,
Pinochet's moustache was made by the
CIA. You pawned your watch here to buy

flowers that wilted in your hands when
the gates remained sealed. Dogs barked
as dogs here did, as dogs in Hebron do
to alert sleepy girls of approaching
patrols, but in Hebron, gods shoot dogs

for their sport. Lost, confused, unable
to locate your home: where to start, end?
Here, you learned to trust all but yourself.
A million sad memories between
Gaza and Santiago. Poems you wrote

disappeared with the key to your hotel
room, where on a white cloth napkin you
penned your heart, folded it gently, placed
it in the nightstand: *Poets should never die
twice, not even here in Santiago.*

LULLABY

I'll etch your name
on a secret star
we'll both go there
on frightful nights

when Mother Earth
runs out of room
for you and me

I'll hold you tight
and sing you songs
of a distant land
beyond the stars

and watch you grow
between my heart
and the highest high

I'll draw your face
on a single seed
and hold your palm
to face the sun

when you're awake
and call out my name
don't moan or cry

I'll return
to raise your hand
at a shooting star
and wish for you

another day
another sun
another world

where Palestine
is a mountain top
of soil and air
and a purple sky

For (Miriam),
a refugee child from Palestine

BREATHING

That distance
all that distance
can be bridged
by a touch

that pain
all that pain
can be breached
knowing you meant
every word even when
you ceased to talk

tomorrow
all tomorrows
can only happen if
I know you are breathing
just breathing
and I am yet to die

I heard nothing for so long
I wondered
are you really you
will you ever come back?

Sitting still I thought
maybe you never existed
poetry was just a cruel joke

and the music
all the music
shed crocodile tears
persistently

Words that were
or are yet to be
belong to a language
any language

I am destined
to dream shadows
on grey walls

OPEN YOUR EYES

Beyond the shadow
A man incomplete
Stubborn voice
Soul fresh
With grief and hope

Open your heart
World beneath the skin
Is unquenchable
Secrets yet to be revealed

Open your mind
Golden hair
Icy pillow
Rowdy stars
Endless journey
Muffled bliss

Open your hand
Clasp mine
Give me a sign
Resume a forlorn mission
Will the world be happy
Again

Open your mouth
Whisper a word
Just one word
In a language
No one understands
Not even me

Stand up
Move about
Shout out
Will the universe
Obey to reach
The unreachable

O Sun –
Cast a strange hue
New kind world
A curious rhyme
Friends waiting
An empty chair
The horizon

MY NAME IS HERMAN WALLACE

I am a black Palestinian,
South African,
Vietnamese...
My name is Mohammed,
Fatima,
Wallace,
Mandela,
Durra
King ...
Resistance is my creed.
Prophets found their sanctity when
they were shot on my soil.
By Israeli bullets
In the Battle of Dien Bien Phu
And just when you think I am defeated,
My fist will rise from the charred earth,
In a painting by Naji Ali,
Through the thick walls of Louisiana State Penitentiary
In the streets of Hanoi,
Amid the rubble of a Gaza mosque.
Even on my dying bed.
I speak many tongues,
And have many names.
But my face is always my face.
On my forehead stitched the memory of pain.
I smile still.
And teach my son to never hate
Because hate is not love
And love is freedom.
I am a Palestinian.
My name is Herman Wallace
And I will always die free.

YOUR BODY IS A MAP OF THE WORLD'S COLLECTIVE SHAME

Hamza, every savage flash scorches my eyes.
Help me see the afterglow, Hamza.

"My silent prayer will keep the heavens
From falling" Hamza screamed, and I said,

"My muted tears will keep your heart
From breaking. We must not flee, for

The fear in our hearts has vanished.
Our secret bond will annex the stars"

Hamza, what is the color of the sky,
'Where should the birds fly?'

(Ramzy Baroud)
(Edited by Rafiq Kathwari)

 # JEHAN BSEISO

Mama was born on the beach in Gaza and I was born in a hospital room in Los Angeles. I was raised in Jordan and I studied in Lebanon from where I received a Master of Arts in Literature. In 1982, my mother had to leave Lebanon due to the war. In 2006, my sisters and I were also forced to evacuate from Beirut during another Israeli war.

I visited Palestine for the first time in 2012. I'm the only member of my family who was able to return even if it was only for a few days.

I started writing short stories, but eventually gravitated to poetry. I am working on a collection of poems titled, *Conversations Continued*. I think of it as a compilation of real, misheard, and misremembered conversations – always interrupted, never really complete or closed.

There's a chapter dedicated to Palestine, titled *Conversations Homeland* but the truth is, that my personal is political, and is Palestinian. A poem can be about coffee and a broken heart as well as exodus.

Since 2008 I have been working with Médecins Sans Frontières/ Doctors Without Borders. My work has taken me to countries like Afghanistan, Pakistan, Iraq, Ethiopia and others. In all my travels and encounters, I've experienced how support and understanding of the Palestinian cause can cross borders and traverse barriers of culture and language. From my base in Egypt now, I've never physically been closer to Gaza, and one day I know, I will not only write about it but also from Gaza.

GAZA, FROM THE DIASPORA

PART ONE
28.7.2014

I
Even from space Gaza is on fire, is
Children, sheltering in UNRWA schools (hit), is,
Entire families huddled in hospitals (hit), is
You sitting perfectly still in the dark, hoping this one,
Will miss you.

II
From Amman, from Beirut, in Chicago.
We, online, yes.
But no 146 characters this.
1000 killed, 4000 injured, thousands displaced no place.

III
Twitter feeds and Facebook timelines and
10 reasons why you should boycott Israel Now, and
5 Ways Children Die in Gaza today or
How to Lose 18 members of Your Family in One Minute
(@Bibi54 stop saying the rockets are in the damn hospitals, in
the school rooms, under the beds of four year olds)
Maybe it helps that 8 Celebrities Expressed Their Outrage.
tweeted and deleted.
(@CNN@Foxnews Bas rewriting history, Bas lies on tv)
@Jon Stewart, thank you for educating the silent majority
with satire.

IV
Day 17: What happened? What is still happening?
In Jabaliya, the dead console the dying;
Anisa, with one child in her arms, and another in her belly (dead).
In the hospital, they put the pregnant women alone, because they're carrying hope, because they don't want them to see what can happen to children.
Oh white phosphorous (and unconfirmed reports of illegal dense inert metal explosives).

V
I can confirm this:
International law, is clearly for internationals only.
By now, a 7 year old in Gaza has survived 3 wars already, and you're still talking about talks, and sending John Kerry to the Middle East, and thanking Egypt for facilitating nothing.
There's more blood than water today in Gaza.

GAZA, FROM THE DIASPORA

PART TWO
14.08.2014

I
Today in Jabaliya, Khan Younis, in Rafah and Shujaiya,
We are still burying the dead we find, but the living ask:
Wayn Nrouh?
(where to now)
Shu Nsawyi?
(what to do now)
Samidoun; means we last.

II
Habeebi, today you reminded me we under the same sky.
But Nowhere refuge. Only refugees.
Skip breakfast with militias in Benghazi, have lunch in Homs under the rubble.
Leave your house in Mosul.
Leave your house in Mosul.
Leave your house in Mosul.
Three times in one week.
Take your body to Beirut, your heart still beating in Aleppo.
Take your body to Amman, your heart still beating in Gaza.
Escape.
Take the death boats from Egypt and Libya to Italy, leave your children on the shore.

III
Arab Offspring forecast is cloudy;
with prospects of unseasonal paradigm shift.
I don't know politics, but something about this brand of terror
tastes like Burger King.
Take back your Jihadis for hire.
Take back your F16s, your drones, your bombs from the sky in
Iraq, in Libya, in Yemen.

IV
Dear Diaspora,
Maybe you have a good job.
You're happy.
You work with Pepsi.
You work at Memac and Ogilvy.
You don't know if they will close the Novartis head office in
Beirut tomorrow because
another bomb went off.
You don't take cabs in Cairo anyway.
You don't want to move to Dubai like everybody.

V
Dear Diaspora,
Boycott.
Don't sponsor occupation with your Jordanian Dinars,
Dirhams, Dollars and Pound Sterling.

VI
Habeebi, I thought you lost my number, turns out you lost your legs,
On the way to the hospital from Khan Younis to Jabaliya to Rafah.
The border is closed, but my heart tunnel.

RE: CEMETERIES IN PALESTINIAN CAMPS SHORT ON SPACE/DAILY STAR/16.05.12*

And so, the cemeteries are full –
In Lebanon, Jordan, Syria and Gaza.
We will soon bury Palestinians above ground.
Nowhere to live and now,
No quiet place to die, with dignity.
Raise high the beams – carpenters, death architects.
Soon, your walls will reach the sky.

* Title reflects format of an email response to a real news article.

BRAINSTORMING NAKBA

At curious four I asked my mother why Superman did not speak the same language I did
She told me that
Our cartoon hero is a little boy forever ten
His hands clasped behind his back, invisible handcuffs
She told me I had to learn another alphabet, another geography,
In the Big Yellow Atlas, for kids, full of pictures
We stenciled in your awkward shape into maps that didn't even want you
We had to learn your name in their language
They told me I spoke funny.
So I rinsed my accent at school; madraseh instead of madrasa
I read about diaspora and exile and power structures
Without knowing what they meant
So you're American? On paper
And Jordan? Is what I know
And Gaza? An old wives tale
We are bastard children of hyphens and supplements and sentences that start with
Originally I'm from…
At home,
Baba counted in dead bodies, in ratios, and for breakfast we had
Nostalgia and symbols
We read Kanafani, Darwiche and Said
When we found tongues
We learned to speak from the margins of pages,
From the periphery
Maybe this is Freud's "oceanic feeling".
A veritable storehouse in the unconscious
To be from a place and not know the place
There are simpler ways of being in the world, I'm told.
Still I choose Za3tar and Shatta and this awkward Fat7a.

VI

'Because things are the way they are, they will not stay the way they are'
Bertolt Brecht

Baboshka found her voice again after all these years.
Remember Chernobyl? Remember dust?
Yes baby, you dance better than all of them, and baby, you're nuclear.
On the tv, 2010 goes by in flashes; not only war and love/loss but also earthquakes and floods.
Sorry I forgot the milk.
You thought 1994 was your year, habeebi, but I can only think of Rawanda.
I had never seen so many bodies piled up.
They were all arms and legs baby.
Hegel was right, it keeps happening, Srebrenica.
They were all arms and legs.
The day the boots danced into Baghdad my hair was on your pillow.
I was all arms and legs.
I don't know how to tell you this, but history is making fools of us, and I can't just lay here habeebi, with my head on your knees watching the sun come up.

POSTCARDS

Saturday, September 11, 2010

The story is not full bodied.
In our prime, we were tip-toeing around
each other's grammar.
And even long after the full stop, kept going.
Not meaning to, we lost the plot often.
Maps on our backs, long way from home.

Beirut,
May 2008.

TATA'S LOVESONG

I
Maktoob: It is written.
Where?
In a big book in the sky.

II
Tata, my grandmother, would only tell the story in staccato:
"1948. Falasteen. Orange blossom fields. Salt. Blue Gaza waters. " Tears in her long black lashes,
"And when my father died, his horse wept in the funeral".

III
Inhale:
Sikes-Piko, Exodus, memory, shrapnel, black September, blue ribbons on bloodied chests, allahu akbar
Exhale:
Settlements, walls, katyushas, mahmoud darwish, Che Guevara's lips, Jerusalem, Maryam, Kuffieh,

IV
On TV an artist says to the BBC camera:
"This is post-post-post modern. It's actually Andy Warhol, meets Baudrillard, who fucks Jalal El Din Rumi while Derrida looks on. The theme is keys, like, existential symbols. These people left with their keys around their necks. It's 3 dimensional: denial, delusion, deference. The photos are taken from maximum empathy angles…you feel what they feel."
Woman stares at the BBC camera, says:
"I am from Hebron, my house is at the corner of the big street. You know which one I'm talking about? The one with the flower shop and Abu Ali's bakery, next to the girls' high school. You have to taste Abu Ali's bread.
Take two:
"My name is Samia, I walked from Hebron to Jerusalem to Jordan, and these are my keys. I hope to go back someday. Abu Ali, if you're watching this, I just want to say that I've never tasted bread like yours.
Take three:
"My name is Samia, I left Hebron in the dead of night with a small parcel tied around my belly and my keys in a necklace around my neck. One day, I hope to go back to… get out of my face. Get out of my face."

V
This trilogy has only 2 parts: beginning and end.
I put my head on your chest and wait for the summer to become winter again,
Poppies in our hair, elegies on our lips.

GAZA, 2009

No matter white flag.

No matter medicine.
No matter civilian.

No matter international community.

No matter your international waters.

No matter your sanctions, no matter your rhetoric and foreign policy.

Only 62 years' status quo.
Everyday, everyday Nakba.
Subsidized settlements.

Even more walls.

Children on the ICRC bus, visiting their Baba's in your prisons –
Matter.

Food and medicine rotting at every border –
Matter.
From the shadows, the silent majority watch water go on fire.

BIRTH AT THE CHECKPOINT

Israeli soldier puts his weapon down to help Um Ali spread her legs, her face is red with shame, her husband is waiting at home in Abu Dis, he doesn't have the right papers with the blue and white stamps, he can't cross to Jerusalem.

The international community is having 9 course dinners in the Alps.

(In the room the women come and go, talking about the status quo).

She said: He doesn't have the right papers,
So when I drive past the checkpoint into Jerusalem I leave him behind the wall.

I leave him forever each time.

(In the room, the women come and go, talking about the status quo).

A bus of tourists from far far away is at the foot of the sycamore tree in Jericho, they are coming for the tree, they can't smell occupation.

From the little village behind the wall, Jerusalem is beyond the sun.
(In the room, the women come and go, talking about the status quo)

In the old city, you must have knaffeh from the place around the corner, and don't go to,
and buy from,
and eat that,
and bring something back for us, even if it is just a handful of sand.

I'm drinking a mint tea as I listen to an American tour guide give a Jewish family an alternative version of history.

(I was asked several times if I was Israeli, they look like us, or, we look like them)

I don't know.

In the evening, the women of Abu Dis gather around plates of rice and meat, they have seen better days and worse. Some of them will never see Jerusalem again.

(tastes like homeland)

From my window, I can see the largest settlement, Maali Adumeem,
an island on top of the mountain.

takes clean water, gives back sewage.

Around it, the olive trees have been decapitated, a landscape of headless bodies stuck in soil.

WRITING SYRIA

Give me an example. I need a headline.
"Barrel Bombs Cause Mass Evacuations in East Aleppo."
Now put it in a sentence.
"This olive soap comes from Aleppo".
More, go further.
"I lost my God in Aleppo, when I saw the crimes done in the name of Islam".
Mothers cradle the heads of children, fathers look for bodies in the rubble.
Mothers sing to the heads of children, fathers look for little shoes under the rubble.
Mothers cry on the heads of children, fathers try to remember their names.

LETTER TO GHASSAN KANAFANI ON THE 66TH ANNIVERSARY OF THE NAKBA

Dear Ghassan,
On our birthday this year I turned 31 and you turned 78. Even the dead grow old without a homeland.
Do you know that we live and die in diaspora now? Do you know that Palestinian refugee camps are swollen with Iraqis and Syrians now?
Too many Jihadi songs end with the refrain "For Falasteen", but Baba says terrorists can't read maps.
The march to Jerusalem doesn't start from Kunduz. And I definitely cannot see Haifa from Cairo ya "Ansar Beit el Maqdis".
Last week in Beirut I went to the races for the first time and bet $5 on a horse named Thawra.
She lost.
But I met a little boy who said he was from Sabra.
In Jordan, Syrian children say they come from Zaatari and Azraq, not anymore Homs or Hama.
Little boys shouldn't come from refugee camps.

Dear Ghassan,
I've been thinking a lot about whether it's easier to start and stay with nothing than to lose everything from one day to the next. "Always already" - without. 66 years expelled.
Pain is fresh in Syria, Lebanon, Egypt, Libya but our story is old. I was nine when I first realized I shared my birthday with someone else. On the 9th of April, each year the public library ran dotty black and white reels of your life, and afterwards we had cake. I was always curious why you were not showing up at our birthday party. Only years later I realized it was a commemoration not a celebration, or a little bit of both.

Dear Ghassan,
I feel the same way about the Nakba. Everyday Nakba. Each year marks death, dispossession and occupation but also birth, and the celebration of memory and resistance.

Yours,
Jehan

15 May 2014

SARTOR RESARTUS OR THE TAILOR RE-TAILORED

I will wear this dress.

Even if I have nowhere to take it to other than this bad place of waiting.

Behind blinking computer screens.

Pale under harsh white light, after sun has left my skin.

Objects in this mirror appear happier than they are in real life.

Pink cheeks and white teeth.
Fruit and fibre.

Tension is deep tissue now, leaving me anxious at the cellular level.

I used to fall apart with a big bang.
Now I rip like a stuffed doll split neatly down the spine seam.

I won't make a mess, so I will wear this dress.

Antakya, March 2014

CEASEFIRE

Little men, cross legged, trade war stories like boys trade baseball cards.

These are times ripe and full with want and promise never fulfilled.

This much is true:
Lost boys become lost men.

Too much water, too much blood dilutes history and
We always end up with less than what we started.

In Gaza,
There is no legacy under the rubble, no pride in long fires
Burning.

There is a face at the window, sallow.

One woman sighing, her body bears the marks of all their trudging, thighs transformed to gallows and trenches.

Her hair shrouds the dead from both sides and her lap cradles aporias generations can't understand.

HASHTAG GAZA

To the children who lost their lives, and the parents who had to bury them.

Bring your camera.
Bring your candles and spotlights to highlight.
Bring your focus to hashtag anniversary.

Everyday Gaza.

Bring your reporters, your journalists, your moving infographics.

Write:

"Abu Muhammad sits on the balcony, cradling the head of Muhammad.
Sorry.
"The photo of the head of Muhammad."

Talk about bomb shelters and war sirens in Sderot and Tel Aviv.
Call it "Neutrality"

Talk about your 5 dead and your iron dome.
Call it "Objective Reality"

Bring your billion dollar pledges and your aid caravans
Your excel sheets, monitoring reports and donor requirements.
Call it "Accountability".

Write:

"Abu Muhammad sits on the balcony hopelessly, smokes a hopeless cigarette talks about lack of hope."

This one is a human interest story.

And when we invite you into our rubble homes for tea and bread you call it "Generosity."

And when we are strong about our suffering you call it "Resilience."

Write:

51 days.
2,000 dead.
10,000 wounded.

Abu Muhammad says:

My boys took a ball to the beach.
Came back bodies.

How can we remember what we can't forget?

Dr VACY VLAZNA
Editor

I came with my parents, political refugees from the Russian occupation of Czechoslovakia, to Australia. I feel privileged to be the editor of *I remember My Name*. Ironically, I disliked poetry at school, yet my PhD was on the poetry of Wallace Stevens. I love my life as a mother, teacher, and activist, as Coordinator of Justice for Palestine Matters, Human Rights Advisor to the GAM team in the second round of the 2005 Acheh peace talks, Helsinki. I was also convenor of the East Timor Justice Lobby, as well as serving the courageous and finally free East Timorese with UNAMET and UNTAET from 1999–2001.

········ **DAVID BORRINGTON**

David Borrington is a highly accomplished social and political artist producing masterly and distinctive artwork in direct response to current social and world affairs that aims to support the growth of true democracy.

His unique individuality and vision he attributes to, 'I am lucky enough to have severe dyslexia and dyspraxia with a reading and writing age of about a six-year-old.' This allows him to view the world in his own way by bypassing written propaganda. He suffers with short-term memory problems: his mind and thoughts are processed in his long-term memory allowing time to refine and rationalise the masses of data and information of contemporary media which bombards us 24/7, never giving us a moment to think. He is also in the top 0.4% of the population for visual recognition which gives him a natural ability to translate ideas and poetry into the visual arts.

David is managing director of Dekkle Printmaking Studios Ltd. He received his MA from the Royal College of Art in Fine Art Printmaking in 2008. In 2007, he was commissioned by the British government to produce artwork for the 50 year anniversary of the signing of the Treaty of Rome which is in a permanent collection in Chatham House, London.

David was made the official artist by the lawful government of Hawaii in 2013, where he was commissioned to produce a body of work exploring their incredible feat of reforming their lawful government by the Hawaiian Kingdom and international law, which is now recognised by the UN.

GLOSSARY

SAMAH

Imra'a
Imra'a: Arabic for woman.
Watan: homeland
Alommo madrasaton: "A mother is a school"
Inna kaydakonna azeem: "Your guile is great" from the Quranic verse that refers to part of the story of Joseph when the Pharaoh's wife was trying to seduce him.
Hoor alyn: Beautiful women with wide eyes in paradise

Defying the Universe
Alhamdollelah: Arabic meaning "Praise to God".
Mamoul: Arabic sweets made during special times.
Eid: Arabic meaning festival or holiday. Eid al-Fitr the Feast of Breaking the Fast that marks the end of Ramadan. Eid al-Adha or Greater Eid is the Feast of the Sacrifice.
Meramiah: Sage tea.

Words
Hasbaranites: People who promote Israel's false propaganda (hasbara).
Nakba: Meaning 'catastrophe' refers to the 1948 ethnic cleansing of Palestine when Jewish militia systematically destroyed over 500 Palestinian villages from which 750,000 Palestinian refugees were forced to flee to camps in the West Bank, Gaza, Lebanon, Jordan, and Syria, Israel refuses the refugees their inalienable right of return.
Naksa: Naksa Day, the Day of the Setback, is commemorated on the 5th June marking the second displacement of the Palestinian people and the beginning of the Israeli occupation after the Six-Day War in 1967.

RAMZY

Sand and Tears
Sahel: The Sahel region: a belt up to 1,000 km (620 miles) wide that spans the 5,400 km in Africa from the Atlantic Ocean to the Red Sea

Nakba
Thoub: the Arabic word for 'a garment'. A woman's loose fitting traditional robe with
sleeves.
Haifa: The city's name is derived from the Canaanite Arabic word *al-Hayfah*. Built on the slopes of Mt Carmel it was ethnically cleansed by Zionist militias in 1947 when all Haifa's industries, farms, buses, cars, railroads, cattle, real states, private properties became the property of the "Jewish state".
Martyrs Graveyard: The graveyard that bordered Ramzy Baroud's family home in Nuseirat refugee camp, Gaza and where his older brother, Anwar, who died at two years of age from starvation and lack of medicine, is buried.
Jaffa: Jaffa was the largest city in historic Palestine famous worldwide for its citrus fruit, particularly oranges as well as glass, textiles, sweets and metalwork. It was ethnically cleansed by Zionist militia in 1948, the majority of its Palestinian population was pushed into the sea. Jaffa became a suburb of Tel Aviv.

Where are the Noble Poets of Santiago
Santiago: The capital of Chile
Neruda: Palbo Neruda, 1904–73, Chilean poet, diplomat and politician who won the Nobel Prize for Literature in 1971. Gabriel Garcia Marquez called him "the greatest poet of the 20th century in any language".
Allende: Salvador Allende, 1908–73, Chilean physician, politician and first elected Marxist President. He implemented a socialist program for housing health, education, cultural endeavours as well as raising the minimum wage, the nationalisation of

major industries and redistribution of wealth. The US financed his political opposition. He was overthrown and murdered in a military coup indirectly supported by the CIA.

Pinochet: Augusto Pinochet, 1915-2005, succeeded Allende and headed the military jnta that ruled Chile and brutally suppressed the leftist opposition. Pinochet's victims numbered over 40,000 including 3065 disappeared and killed. He was indicted for human rights violations and placed under house arrest in London and later implicated in Chile in over 300 criminal charges. He died while under house arrest.

My Name is Herman Wallace
Herman Wallace: 1941–2013, an innocent man incarcerated for more than 40 years in solitary confinement in Louisiana State Penitentiary for the alleged murder of a prison guard His conviction was overturned three days before he died of cancer. While in prison he joined the Black Panther movement.
Durra: Mohammad Al-Durrah (al-Dura) a 12 years old Gazan boy was cold-bloodedly killed in 2000 by Israeli military fire when he was taking cover with his father. His father was badly wounded and an ambulance driver, Bassam al-Bilbeisi, who tried to rescue them was also killed. Israel first accepted then denied responsibility.
Naji Ali: Naji al-Ali, 1938–1987, Palestinian political cartoonist and journalist who was scathingly critical of the USA, Arab regimes, the corrupt Palestinian leadership and the Israeli occupation. He created Handala, the eternal Palestinian refugee child who stood as a witness in his cartoons. Naji was shot in the face on a London street and died five weeks later.

Your Body is a Map of the World's Collective Shame
Hamza: Little Hamza Mus'ab Almadani of Khan Younis, Gaza, was hit by illegal phosphorus bomb pellets on 25 July 2014 during Israel's war on Gaza. His body has a map of horrific tissue damage from the burning of phosphorus through his 3 year old skin.
Rafiq Kathwari I thank you for editing my poetry, from Ramzy

JEHAN

Brainstorming Nakba
little boy forever ten: Handala, created by Palestinian political cartoonist, Naji al-Ali, is the eternal refugee child who is a symbol of Palestinian identity, resistance, and the right of return
Madraseh , madrasa: Arabic for school.
Kanafi: Ghassan Kanafani,1936–1972, Palestinian writer, poet, editor and active member of the Popular Front for the Liberation of Palestine and the PLO. He was assassinated by the Mossad by a car bomb in Beirut.
Darwich – Mahmoud Darwish, 1941–2008, Palestine's national poet.
Said – Edward Said, 1935–2003, Palestinian American literary theorist and intellectual. He advocated Palestinian independence and political and human rights.
Za3tar: Zatar, the dried thyme that Palestinians in general eat with everything.
Shatta: A hot pepper paste added to food and is notoriously Gazan.
Fat7a: An upward inflection at the end of words, that is Egyptian/Gazan.. it is the "ah" sound instead of the ""eh". For example madra(sa) – school-madras(eh)
Habeebi: Arabic for "my love", "darling"

Tata's Lovesong
Tata: Grandmother
Maktoob: "It is written" signifying whatever happens is known to God.
Sikes-Piko: Sykes Picot Agreement signed secretly between the governments of te United Kingdom and France dividing the Middle Eastern Ottoman Empire between them in violation of guarrantees of Arab independence.
Allahu akbar: God is great.
Falesteen: Palestine
Katushas: Russian rocket launchers

Kuffieh: A square cotton scarf with a distinctive checkered pattern that has become symbolic of Palestinian nationalism.
Baudrillard: Jean Baudrillard. 1929–2007, French philosopher, cultural theorist and political commentator.
Jalal El Din Rumi: 13th century Persian poet and Sufi mystic.
Derrida: Jacques Derrida, 1930–2004, French Algerian philosopher. Founder of 'deconstruction'.

Birth at The Checkpoint
Knaffeh: a goat cheese pastry soaked in a sweet sugar syrup.
Abu Dis: An ancient Palestinian village 2 kilometres from the Old City of Jerusalem and cut off from Jerusalem by the illegal Annexation Wall.
Maali Adumeem: Ma'ale Adumin is an Israeli colony/settlement built on stolen Palestinian land and held illegal under international law. The Sodastream plant is located there and for that reason is targeted by the Boycott Divestment and Sanctions (BDS) movement.

Letter to Ghassan Kanafani on the 66th Anniversary of the Nakba
Ghassan Kanafani; the famous Palestinian journalist, novelist, and short story writer, whose writings were deeply rooted in Arab Palestinian culture, inspired a whole generation during and after his lifetime, both in word and deed. In 1972, he and his niece, Lamis were assassinated by Israeli agents in Beirut.
Kunduz: Northern province of Afghanistan
ya "Ansar Beit el Maqdis": (translated as Supporters of Jerusalem) is an active militant group operating in the Sinai Peninsula.
Thawra: Arabic world for revolution.
Zaatari and Azraq: Regions in Jordan where the United Nations has set up some of the largest refugee camps for Syrians.

Ceasefire
aporias: internal contradiction that is impossible to resolve

Hashtag Gaza
My boys took a ball to the beach: Ahed Atef Bakr, 10, Zakariya Ahed Bakr, 10, Mohammad Ramiz Bakr, 11, and Ismail Mahmoud Bakr, 9, were killed playing football on 16 July 2014 when Israeli forces shelled a beachfront in the Gaza Strip. The Israeli military responsible were exonerated by Israel.

novum PUBLISHER FOR NEW AUTHORS

The publisher

> **Whoever stops getting better, will in time stop being good.**

This is the motto of novum publishing, and our focus is on finding new manuscripts, publishing them and offering long-term support to the authors.
Our publishing house was founded in 1997, and since then it has become THE expert for new authors and has won numerous awards.

Our editorial team will peruse each manuscript within a few weeks free of charge and without obligation.

You will find more information about
novum publishing and our books on the internet:

www.novum-publishing.co.uk